**Mapping Britain's Landscapes**

# Rivers

Barbara Taylor

## W
### FRANKLIN WATTS
LONDON • SYDNEY

First published in 2007 by Franklin Watts

Franklin Watts
338 Euston Road
London NW1 3BH

Franklin Watts Australia
Level 17/207 Kent Street
Sydney, NSW 2000

Series editor: Sarah Peutrill
Art director: Jonathan Hair
Design: White Design
Picture research: Diana Morris
Consultant: Steve Watts
Additional map illustrations: John Alston

A CIP catalogue record for this book is
available from the British Library.

Dewey number: 526.09141
ISBN: 978 0 7496 7111 2

Printed in China

Franklin Watts is a division of
Hachette Children's Books, an
Hachette Livre UK company.

## RIVER SAFETY
**Rivers can be dangerous places.
Always follow the safety advice
of a teacher or other adult and stay
well away from fast-flowing water.**

Picture credits: Altos Mapping: 9. Courtesy of
the Elan Valley Visitor Centre: 25. © ESA 2003:
15. Paul Glendell/PD: 5. Jason Hawkes/Corbis:
front cover, 19. John Heseltine/Corbis: 8. Richard
Klune/Corbis: 20t. Mike Lane/Still Pictures: 24.
Brian Moyes/PD: 22. Ordnance Survey © Crown
copyright 2007: 23. Ordnance Survey © Crown
copyright 2007 supplied by
mapsinternational.co.uk: front cover l, 4, 11, 13,
17, 18, 21, 29. Peter Smith Photography: 16.
John Sparks/Corbis: 10. Topfoto: 20b. Adam
Woolfitt/Corbis: 1, 6. David Wootton/PD: 12.
Every attempt has been made to clear copyright.
Should there be any inadvertent omission please
apply to the publisher for rectification.

**Note to parents and teachers:** Every effort has
been made by the Publishers to ensure that the
websites in this book are suitable for children,
that they are of the highest educational value,
and that they contain no inappropriate or
offensive material. However, because of the
nature of the Internet, it is impossible to
guarantee that the contents of these sites will
not be altered. We strongly advise that Internet
access is supervised by a responsible adult.

# Contents

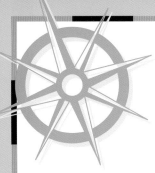

# Mapping rivers

Rivers are channels of fresh water that flow downhill from high ground to low ground, often pouring into the sea. There are around 20,000 rivers in Britain, which flow through many types of landscape and settlement.

## Maps and photographs

→ A map can tell you much more about a river than a photograph.

→ A photograph of a river is complicated and shows a lot of details, which are difficult to interpret. A map of a river is a simple picture, seen from above. It highlights important information about the river.

→ A photograph may just show you what a river looks like, while a map helps you to answer questions, such as: "How has the river changed the land?" or "How do people use the river?"

→ Photographs of rivers all have a similar style, while maps can be drawn in many ways to show different kinds of information.

## MAPS AND RIVERS

Maps show us where rivers flow and how they are used. They don't show things that move around, such as boats or people, just the things that are there all the time. It's impossible to mark everything on a map, so mapmakers choose the most important features of the river. Maps use colours, lines and special shapes called symbols to mark the positions of river features. Look at the key on the side of a map to find out what the colours, lines and symbols mean.

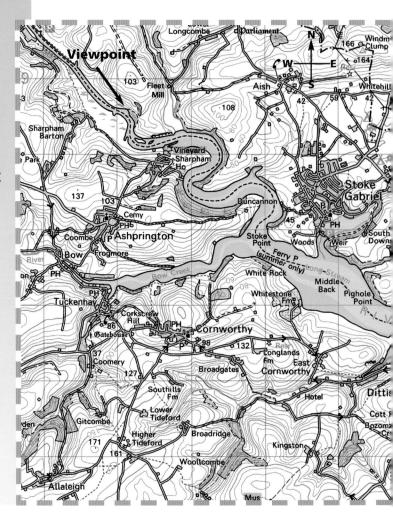

## MAPS OF BRITAIN

There are many types of map, such as landscape maps, road maps, weather maps, tourist maps, world maps and maps of shopping centres. Books of maps are called atlases. You can look up places in an atlas index and find the square on the map where the place is located. (See pages 14/15 for more about finding places on maps.)

The most useful maps for finding out about Britain's river landscapes are Ordnance Survey (OS) maps, like the one opposite. This book shows you how to understand OS maps and other maps, and how they can reveal the features of rivers.

On a map, north is usually at the top, south is at the bottom, west is on the left and east is on the right. To help you remember this, make up a rhyme going clockwise around the compass, such as, "Never Enjoy Slimy Waffles".

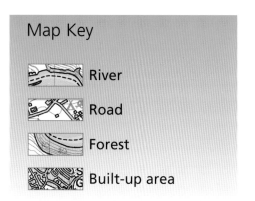

### Map Key

River

Road

Forest

Built-up area

↑ **This is the River Dart, winding its way through the countryside of South Devon, in the south west of Britain. Compare the shape of the river on the photograph with the river on the map. South is at the top of the photo but at the bottom of the map. The viewpoint is marked on the map with an arrow showing the direction.**

# Rivers and the water cycle

The water in rivers comes from precipitation, such as rain, that falls from the sky. This makes rivers part of the water cycle, which is the movement of water from the sky to the land or sea and back to the sky again. The water cycle has no beginning and no end. It keeps recycling all the water so the amount of water on the Earth always stays the same.

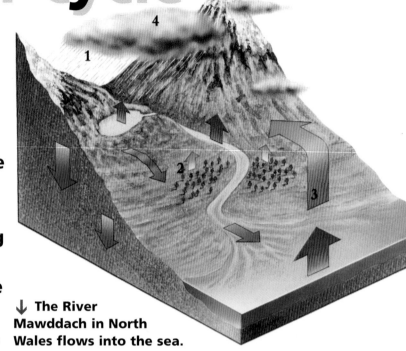

↓ The River Mawddach in North Wales flows into the sea.

## LOOK AT THE DIAGRAM AND PHOTO (LEFT)

**1** Precipitation falls from clouds and collects in rivers, lakes and oceans.

**2** Water at the surface of rivers, lakes and oceans warms up in the Sun. Some of it turns into an invisible gas called water vapour and disappears into the air. This is called evaporation.

**3** The evaporated water rises up into the air, cools down and turns back into tiny drops of liquid water. This is called condensation.

**4** The condensed water drops collect together to make clouds. When the water drops become too large and heavy to hang in the sky, they fall from the clouds as precipitation. Water collects in the river, ready to begin the cycle all over again.

• Where are some of the parts of the water cycle happening in the photograph?

## TAKING IT FURTHER

Look on the Internet to find out the source of five British rivers. They can be local rivers in your own area, or large rivers such as the Trent, the Severn, the Mersey, the Tweed or the Thames.

➜ **On a weather map, the landscape is not so important. The main features are the symbols used to show features of the weather, such as rain, snow, clouds and sunshine. The numbers indicate the temperature in different areas.**

## Where rivers start

➜ **Rivers begin from rainfall. They always flow downhill from a starting point, called the source. There are four main sources of rivers:**

➜ **1) A natural hollow in the land where water collects.**

➜ **2) A marsh or a lake.**

➜ **3) The end of a melting glacier (a river of ice).**

➜ **4) Underground water that gushes out onto the surface as a spring.**

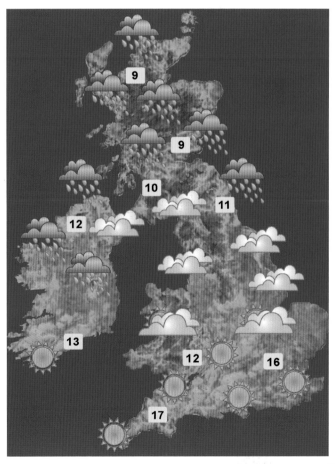

7

# How do rivers change the land?

**River water is pulled downhill by the force of gravity. As the water flows downhill, it wears away the land by loosening or breaking off pieces of rock and soil and carrying them away. This process is called erosion. The river deposits the eroded material in another place.**

## THE EFFECT OF RIVERS ON THE LAND

Rivers erode dips and channels in the land in some places and build up banks and new land in other places. Small streams or smaller rivers called tributaries flow into the main river channel, forming a branching pattern called a drainage pattern. The shape of this pattern depends on the rocks, soil, climate and changes people make to the course of the river.

→ **The Devil's Kitchen area of Snowdonia. The name comes from the clouds, which were said to look like cooking smoke coming out of a chimney. You can see the river water swirling around the rocks and wearing them away.**

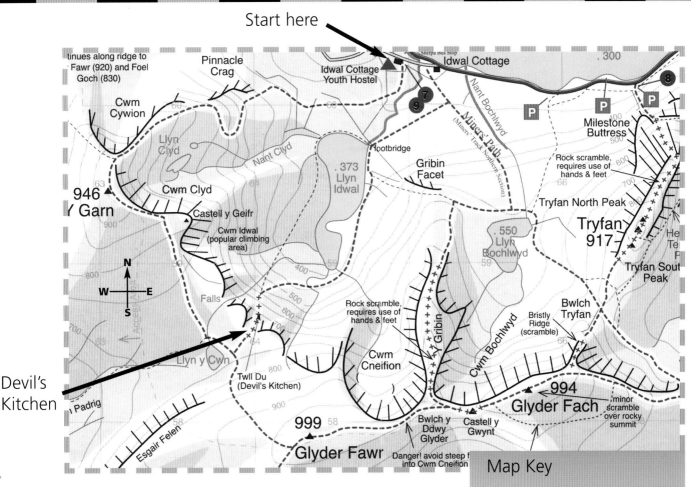

Start here

continues along ridge to
Y Fawr (920) and Foel
Goch (830)

Pinnacle
Crag

Idwal Cottage
Youth Hostel

Sherpa Bus Stop
Idwal Cottage

.300

Cwm
Cywion

Llyn
Clyd

Footbridge

Gribin
Facet

Milestone
Buttress

Rock scramble,
requires use of
hands & feet

Cwm Clyd

.373
Llyn
Idwal

946
Y Garn

Castell y Geifr

Cwm Idwal
(popular climbing
area)

Tryfan North Peak

Tryfan
917

.550
Llyn
Bochlwyd

Tryfan Sout
Peak

N
W E
S

Falls

Rock scramble,
requires use of
hands & feet

Bwlch
Tryfan

Bristly
Ridge
(scramble)

Llyn y Cwn

Cwm
Cneifion

Cwm Bochlwyd

Devil's
Kitchen

Padrig

Twll Du
(Devil's Kitchen)

994
Glyder Fach

minor
scramble
over rocky
summit

Esgair Felen

999

Bwlch y
Ddwy
Glyder

Castell y
Gwynt

Glyder Fawr

Danger! avoid steep f
into Cwm Cneifion

## ↓ Using the map

### Planning routes and looking at scale

This map of Snowdonia shows a high ridge called The Glyders, with the rivers flowing down from the ridge into a number of lakes. Plan a circular walk from the Idwal Cottage Youth Hostel, up onto the ridge through the Devil's Kitchen, along the ridge and back again.

Look at the scale on the map. This shows you how much smaller the mountains are on the map compared with their size in real life. On this map, 1 cm on the map is equal to 250 m in real life.

Maps can be drawn to different scales. Large scale maps like this one show a small area in a lot of detail. Small scale maps show a large area, with very little detail. On an electronic map, you can zoom in and out and view the map at different scales.

### Map Key

Footpath

Cliffs

0 km      **Scale**      1 km

0 cm  1 cm  2 cm  3 cm  4 cm

### TAKING IT FURTHER

Find some large and small scale maps of your area. Which scale is best for the following purposes:

- investigating the rivers of Britain?
- canoeing along a river?
- planning a route by car or train?
- finding a street in a town?

9

# Rivers in the highlands

**Near the source of a river, the water flows fast down steep slopes, which are usually on higher ground or in the mountains – the highlands.**

The water cuts down into the land, carving out a narrow, V-shaped channel. Other characteristic features of rivers in the highlands are waterfalls, foaming "white water" and tongues of land called spurs along the valley sides.

→ **The waterfalls of Sour Milk Gill in the Lake District flow down over a sloping cliff of hard rock. The water has worn away the softer rock below the falls so the river drops down from a great height.**

← **Three-dimensional maps show how the land goes up and down, but they can't be folded up and carried around very easily.**

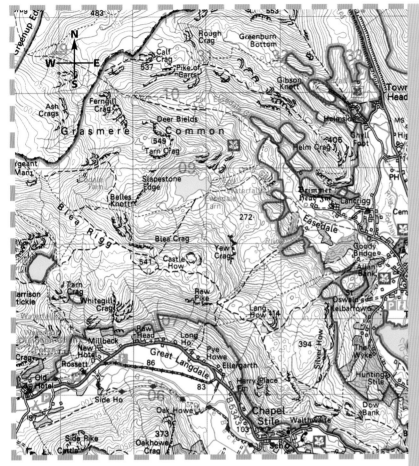

## CONTOUR LINES

One of the main ways of showing the ups and downs of the land on a flat map is by using thin brown lines called contours. Contour lines join up points on the map that are the same number of metres above the sea. When contour lines are close together the slopes are very steep. In a V-shaped valley the contour lines meet at the top of the valley to make a V-shape.

## TAKING IT FURTHER

Find out some other ways of showing height on a map, such as using colour shading.

Lines called hachures may also show height on a map. Find a map with hachures. Are they thicker or thinner on steeper slopes?

## Look at the map

→ This map is of Grasmere Common in the Lake District.

→ Find the blue lines that show the rivers. The brown contour lines around them are close together – showing that the rivers are in steeply sloping valleys.

→ The thick, jagged black lines in some areas mark the edges of rocky cliffs, called crags. Can you find Blea Crag and Yew Crag?

→ The waterfalls in the photograph are in Sour Milk Gill, a valley leading down from Easedale Tarn. Find the waterfalls on the map.

→ Can you imagine what the landscape would look like if you walked up Far Easedale Gill?

→ The height at a particular point on a map is sometimes marked by a spot height. There is one of these spot heights just below Sour Milk Gill. How many metres high is the land at this point?

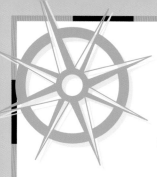

# Rivers in the lowlands

As a river flows from the highlands onto lower ground, it starts to twist and turn, forming loops called meanders. The river cuts sideways into the land, rather than downwards as it did in the highlands. Lots of small streams have now joined the river so the river is wider and flows through a deep channel.

### THE RIVER DEE

The best way to see a river's meanders is in an aerial photograph like this. The map opposite shows the same river, but there is more of the river shown on the map. The small box on the map shows the area you can see on the photograph.

### MEANDERS

When the curve of a river changes direction, it is the start of a new meander. On the outside bend of a meander, the river flows quickly. It eats into the riverbank, carrying material away and forming small cliffs. On the inside bend, the river water flows more slowly. It drops, or deposits, some of the material it is carrying to make ridges of sand and gravel, called bars. Since one riverbank is cut away at the same time as the other bank is filled in, the width of the river stays roughly the same.

## Map Key

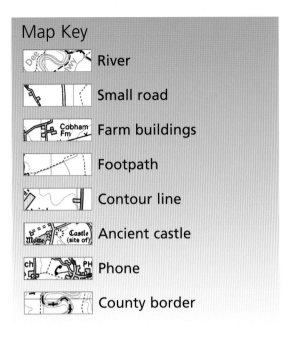

- River
- Small road
- Farm buildings
- Footpath
- Contour line
- Ancient castle
- Phone
- County border

← **The meanders of the River Dee, near Wrexham in Wales.**

# ↓ Using the map

## Symbols

A map uses simple symbols to pick out the main features of an area such as rivers or lakes, as well as features people have built, such as farms and towns. Symbols are simple signs, lines, letters or coloured areas that stand for the real things.

The key (left) shows some of the symbols used on this map of the River Dee. Find each one on the map.

Can you match the River Dee's meanders in the photograph with the meanders on the map?

The border between Wales and England mainly follows the course of the river. Why do you think this is? Why does it sometimes follow a slightly different route?

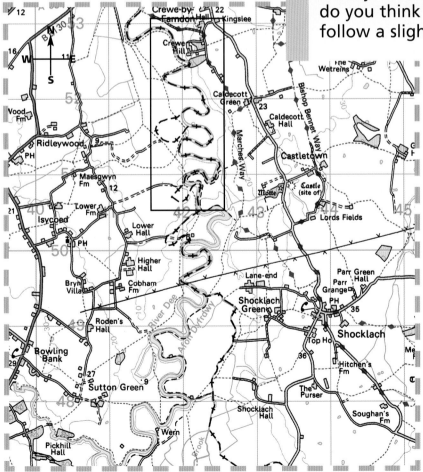

## TAKING IT FURTHER

Find the River Dee in an atlas. Can you name the mountains where it starts and the sea that it flows into?

Follow the River Dee from Farndon (off the top of this map) down to Bangor on Dee (off the bottom of this map). How many meanders can you count on this stretch of the river?

# Where rivers meet the sea

Most rivers end by flowing into the sea. This wide opening is called the river's mouth. If the mouth is very wide, it is also called an estuary. Here, the salty seawater pushes its way up the river with the tide.

## DROPPING MATERIAL

At the mouth the river slows down and drops the particles of sand, gravel and mud that it is carrying. This mud builds up to make mud flats beside the river.

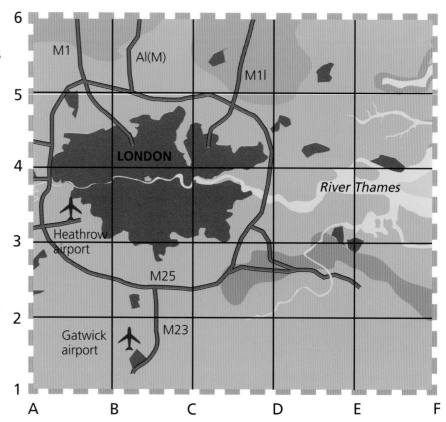

↑ This sketch map is based on the photograph of the River Thames, opposite. It is a simplified version of the photograph, which makes it much easier to see where things are.

## ⬇ Using the map

### Grid references

The map is divided into squares by lines called grid lines. At the end of each grid line is a number or a letter. Grid references help to pinpoint a particular square on the map. They always have the number or letter of the line at the top or bottom of the map first, then the number or letter of the line up the sides of the map. You can remember this by thinking of the phrase: "along the corridor and up the stairs". For example Heathrow Airport is in square A3.

Give the grid reference for the square where the estuary of the River Thames meets the M25.

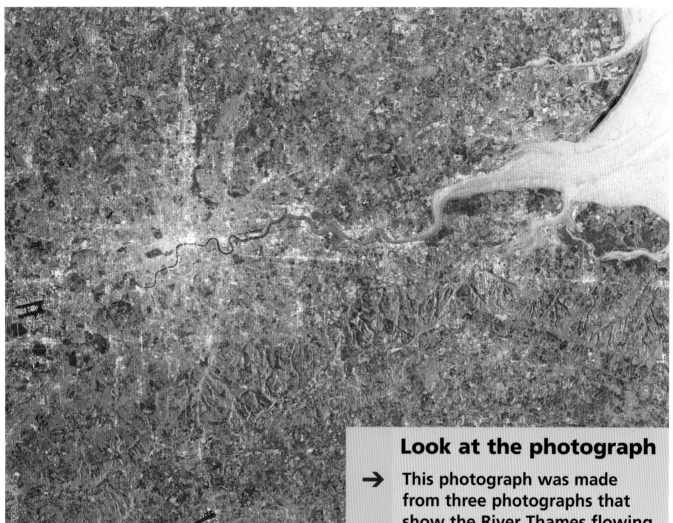

© ESA 2003

## TAKING IT FURTHER

Find the River Thames in an atlas and trace its journey from its source in the Cotswolds of Gloucestershire to the North Sea. The Thames is the longest river in England and millions of people depend on its waters. Find out the total length of the River Thames. Which six counties does the river flow through?

Why do you think the City of London grew up beside the River Thames?

## Look at the photograph

→ This photograph was made from three photographs that show the River Thames flowing through London and into the North Sea. Each photograph has been given a different colour. The photographs were taken from high above the ground looking straight down.

→ Find the big meanders along the river. Where does the river flow into the sea?

→ Can you find two other rivers that flow into the North Sea near the estuary of the River Thames? Look in an atlas to find out their names.

# When rivers flood

Sometimes a river gets too full so some of the water spills over the riverbanks and floods the land nearby. This usually happens in the lowlands, where rivers flow across flatter land, called the river's floodplain. Floods damage crops, buildings and bridges and put the lives of people and animals at risk.

## WHY DO FLOODS HAPPEN?

- Very heavy rainfall or a lot of snow melting suddenly in spring.
- High tides on the coast causing flooding at the mouth of a river.
- People making changes to the natural course of a river, such as cutting down lots of trees, or draining marshes which soak up water.
- Water draining quickly from concrete surfaces in towns and cities and filling up rivers too fast.

↑ A flooded section of the River Ouse in York in 2000. The floods were caused by extreme weather.

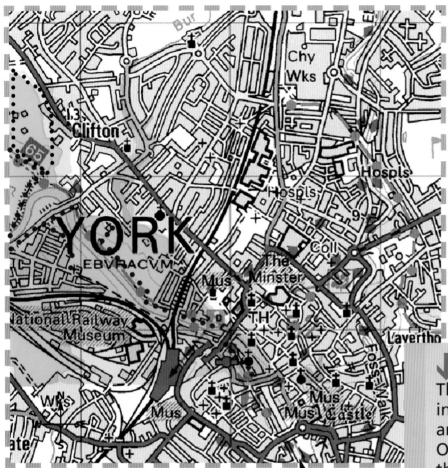

↑ **Maps, like this one of York, predict the risk of flooding. They help people to plan for future floods and decide where to build houses or factories and farm the land safely.**

**River Ouse**

**TAKING IT FURTHER**
Visit the Environment Agency website and investigate flood risk maps for your area. Go to: www.environment-agency.gov.uk/subjects/flood and type in your postcode. You could also create a project folder on severe floods in recent years.

## ↓ Look at the map

This map provides information about flood risks and flood defences. The River Ouse is just north and east of the Railway Museum.

Dark blue shows the natural floodplain area that could be flooded if there were no flood defences.

Green shows the extent of a future extreme flood.

The red line shows flood defences, such as walls, embankments and areas to store floodwater.

The black-dotted area near Clifton has flood defences in place. Without the defences, this area would be flooded.

## THE RIVER OUSE

Most of Britain was affected by severe floods in the autumn of 2000, especially in city centres where bridges cross rivers. In York, the floods were the highest for over 350 years. The River Ouse burst its banks after heavy rain and the floodwater caused major damage to hundreds of buildings. Special flood defence walls and thousands of sandbags held back the water, but many people had to be rescued from their homes by boat. The railway line between York and Darlington had to be closed when floods from the River Ouse and the River Derwent covered the railway tracks.

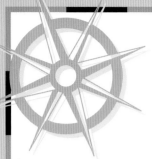

# River settlements

In the past people often settled near rivers because they can be used in so many different ways. Small settlements often grew up at places where rivers were easy to cross or where a river bend surrounded a village, making it easy to defend. Many of these small settlements have grown into Britain's towns and cities.

## Look at the photo and map

→ This map of Marlow has been turned so that it faces the same way as the photo. North on the map is now down the left hand side. Which way is the river flowing?

→ Find Marlow's famous suspension bridge in the photo and on the map.

→ Turn the book to look closely at the map symbols. Where is the weir on the river? And the same on the photo?

→ Can you find a school, a church and a railway station on the map?

→ What leisure interests could you follow in Marlow?

### WHY LIVE NEAR RIVERS?
- People can use the water for drinking and washing.
- Farmers can water their crops or provide water for their farm animals to drink. Crops grow well on the rich soils of river floodplains. These soils are built up from layers of river mud, which the river deposits along its banks in times of flood.
- Fast-flowing rivers can be used to drive machinery or generate electricity (see pages 24–25).

- Rivers are water highways, useful for transporting goods and people.
- People use rivers in their leisure time for activities such as canoeing and fishing.
- At the mouth of some rivers, sheltered, deep-water sites make ideal ports or harbours for fishing, trade or industry.

↑ **This is the town of Marlow, on the River Thames in Buckinghamshire, southern England. Marlow grew up around a bridge over the river and was on a major trade route from London, with barges carrying goods such as corn, oil, paper and wood along the river.**

## FLOOD RISKS

The first settlements were usually built away from marshy areas or places that might flood. Today, there are so many people living in Britain that more and more homes have to be built in areas at risk from river flooding. People also like to build their homes on the flat land near rivers, with a pleasant view.

# Transport and crossing places

Rivers and canals have been used for transporting people and goods for centuries. However, rivers are also barriers to journeys. Small rivers can be crossed at shallow places called fords. Deeper and wider rivers have to be crossed using ferries, bridges or tunnels.

## SatNav

Satellite navigation systems are a special kind of map. In cars they pinpoint exactly where you are by picking up radio signals sent out by a network of satellites out in space. They can be used instead of road maps like the one opposite.

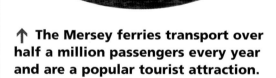

↑ The Mersey ferries transport over half a million passengers every year and are a popular tourist attraction.

### THE RIVER MERSEY

Liverpool grew up at the mouth of the River Mersey, where it flows into the Irish Sea. People have been crossing the River Mersey from Liverpool to Birkenhead by ferry for over 800 years. Nowadays, as well as the ferries there are also three tunnels underneath the river, which provide an alternative means of crossing.

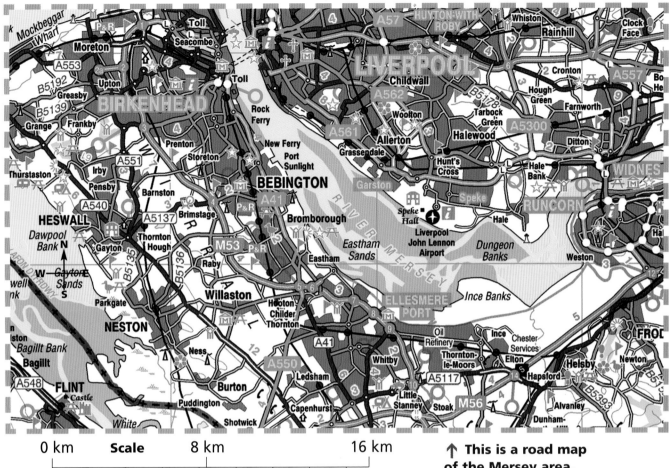

**Scale**

0 km      8 km      16 km

0 cm   1 cm   2 cm   3 cm   4 cm   5 cm   6 cm   7 cm   8 cm

↑ This is a road map of the Mersey area.

## ↓ Using the map

Maps help you find your way to places. If you are going on a journey, it's a good idea to plan your route on a map.

Find the narrow crossing place where the ferries and tunnels cross the Mersey. Imagine all these crossings are not in use. How long would it take you to go all the way round by road, crossing the river at the Runcorn-Widnes bridge? Some of the roads will be A roads and some will be motorways. Measure the total distance using a piece of wool or thin string and a ruler. Then use the map scale to convert this figure into the distance in the real place.

Think about the average speed of a car on these roads and calculate the time the journey takes.

## TAKING IT FURTHER

The River Mersey starts near Stockport and flows westwards for about 112 km until it reaches Liverpool. Trace the course of the River Mersey on an atlas. Look at the map symbols to find out more about the features along the riverbanks. How many settlements are built near the river? Where are the main bridges?

To travel on a virtual tour across the River Mersey, visit www.bbc.co.uk/liverpool/virtual_tours/ferry.shtml.

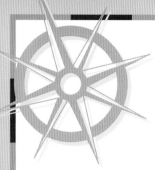

# Water and work

Many of the jobs people do are closely linked to rivers, from farming, forestry and conservation to shipbuilding, power generation and the housing industry. Many heavy industries that used to be located next to urban riversides, such as shipbuilding, have declined and these parts of Britain's rivers are now mainly used for the leisure and tourist industry.

↓ The *Cardigan Bay* warship being built for the British Royal Navy at the BAE Systems shipyard on the River Clyde.

### THE RIVER CLYDE, GLASGOW

The River Clyde is the third longest river in Scotland. It was very important during the Industrial Revolution for trade with the Americas. The river channel was dredged to make it deeper and wider so large ships could navigate all the way into Glasgow. Shipbuilding became the most important industry on the river, with warships and ocean liners being built there.

After the Second World War (1939–45), fewer warships were needed and other shipbuilding countries took work away from the Clyde shipbuilders. Many shipyards closed but today there are still two major shipyards on the Clyde, which make warships such as the one in the photograph.

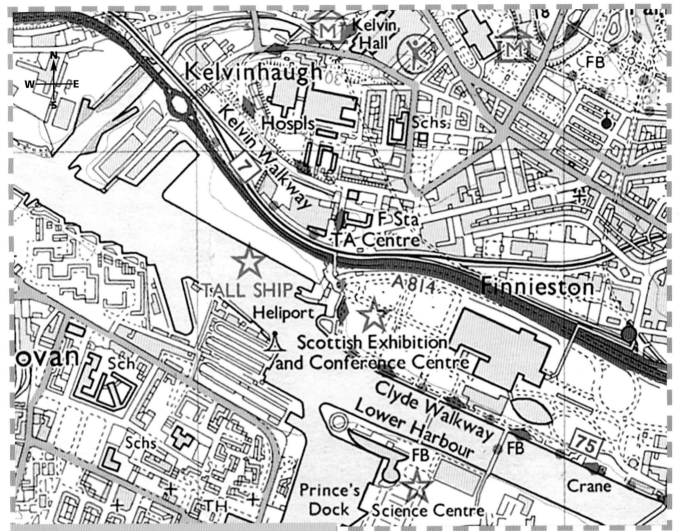

## Look at the map

→ This map shows part of the River Clyde flowing through the docklands of Glasgow.

→ Find the following visitor attractions on the map:
  • Scottish Exhibition and Conference Centre
  • Tall Ship
  • Crane
  • Museum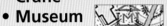

→ What other future uses for the old docklands can you think of?

## CLYDE REDEVELOPMENT

Other dockland areas where ships once unloaded their cargoes are now being used for office blocks, housing, shopping and tourist attractions. The river has also been cleaned up over the last 20 years to make it suitable for leisure use.

## TAKE IT FURTHER

Find out where the River Clyde begins and ends. Find out about the Glasgow Harbour development using the Internet.

# Dams and reservoirs

Dams are very strong, thick walls built across river valleys to control the flow of water. The large lakes that form behind the dams are called reservoirs and they are marked as patches of blue on maps, just like natural lakes. The water stored in the reservoir can be released when it is needed.

↓ The Claerwen Dam in Wales took six years to build and was finished in 1952. It is 56 m high and 355 m long. The reservoir behind the dam holds 483,000 megalitres of water. When the reservoir is full, water overflows down the face of the dam, making a striking waterfall.

## BRITISH DAMS

There are about 2,500 large dams in Britain. They are used to control flooding, generate electricity (hydro-power) and provide a regular water supply for houses, farms, industry and leisure activities on rivers.

## THE ELAN VALLEY DAMS

The four massive dams on the Elan and Claerwen Rivers in Mid Wales were built at the beginning of the 20th century to provide water for the city of Birmingham. At the end of the 20th century, five new hydro-power turbines were hidden underground at the bottom of the original dams to generate electricity. The area is famous for its scenery and wildlife, such as red kites (birds).

## USE AN ATLAS

In an atlas, find the Elan Valley reservoirs in the Cambrian Mountains of Mid Wales. The reservoirs are south east of Aberystwyth, which is in the middle of Cardigan Bay. Look for Llyn (Lake) Brianne, which is south of the Claerwen Reservoir. Which river flows into Llyn Brianne from the north?

Map legend:
- Woodland
- Reservoirs
- Estate Boundary and Watershed
- Roads

Map labels: River Elan, Abergwngu, River Gwngu, River Elan, Pont ar Elan, Nant Hirin, Craig Goch Reservoir, A 470 To Llangurig, To Worcester A44, Pen-y-Garreg Reservoir, B4518, Rhayader, River Claerwen, Filter beds, A 470 To Builth Wells, Elan Village, Claerwen Reservoir, Garreg-Ddu Viaduct, Elan Valley Visitor Centre, River Wye, River Claerwen, Nant-y-Carw, Caban Coch Reservoir, Rhiwnant, Dol y Mynach Dam

## Look at the map

→ **Is the Claerwen Reservoir east or west of the Caban Coch Reservoir?**

→ **Is the visitor centre north or south of the Craig Coch Reservoir? Which is the most southerly reservoir?**

## TAKING IT FURTHER

Hydro-power provides at least 10% of Scotland's energy. Find out about big hydro-power schemes in Scotland such as the Glendoe hydro-power scheme.

Building a dam across a river changes the natural flow of water. What sort of problems do you think this might cause? Think about the effects on wildlife and farming. When the river flows into the reservoir behind the dam, what happens to all the mud and stones it is carrying?

# Rivers and recreation

**From canoeing, rowing and fishing to cycling, painting and photography, many people in Britain choose to spend their leisure time on or near rivers. People enjoy seeing river features, such as waterfalls or the wildlife that depends on rivers.**

## PICTORIAL MAPS

Many tourist maps of rivers are drawn in a pictorial style. This means that little pictures are used to stand for the different leisure features, such as sailing, picnic sites, nature reserves or places to hire boats or bicycles.

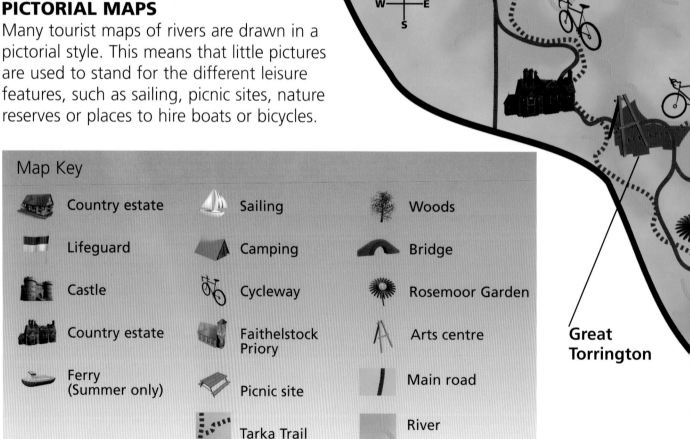

Instow

Northam

Bideford

River Torridge

Great Torrington

N W E S

### Map Key

| | | |
|---|---|---|
| Country estate | Sailing | Woods |
| Lifeguard | Camping | Bridge |
| Castle | Cycleway | Rosemoor Garden |
| Country estate | Faithelstock Priory | Arts centre |
| Ferry (Summer only) | Picnic site | Main road |
| | Tarka Trail | River |

## TIPS ON DRAWING PICTORIAL MAPS:

- This sort of map can be creative, decorative and fun. It doesn't have to be too accurate, just give a general idea of things to do along the river.
- The edge of the map can even be an unusual shape, such as the outline of an otter shown on these two pages.
- Don't worry about scale. The features can be much bigger than they would be on a landscape map.
- Make the picture symbols three dimensional, as if you were looking at them from the ground, not from above.
- Draw simple pictures of things with bold lines, not just outline shapes. The symbols can even be in a cartoon style.
  - Don't include too much detail in the background. Make the pictorial symbols stand out and become the main focus of the map.
    - You could include boxes around the edge of the map with photographs or drawings of each site and more details, such as telephone numbers and opening times.
    - Include a key so people using the map can understand your symbols.

## ↓ Using the map

The map shows the River Torrington in north-west Devon. Beside the river is the Tarka Trail – a walking and cycling trail beside parts of the river featured in Henry Williamson's book, *Tarka the Otter*.

Which town is near the historical bridge across the river? Where is Rosemoor Garden? Where can you catch a ferry across the river? Where can you camp? Which is the best spot to see the biggest river meanders?

## TAKING IT FURTHER

Using an atlas, choose a river in Britain, such as the Thames through London or the Tyne in Newcastle, where there are lots of tourist attractions. Draw a pictorial map of a stretch of the river.

# Check your map skills

Use these two pages to check that you understand the mapping skills introduced in this book. Once you can read a map, you will be able to discover all sorts of information about rivers and how they change the landscape.

## SCALE

Everything on a map is usually reduced down by the same amount to fit onto the map. This is called drawing to scale. The scale of a map tells you how the size of the map compares to the size of the real landscape. You can use the scale to work out the distances between two or more points on the map.

## GRIDS

A map grid is a network of equal squares drawn on top of the map. At the edge of a map, each line has a number or a letter at the end. To give a grid reference, find the numbers or letters at the ends of the two lines that meet in the bottom left-hand corner of a grid square. Refer to the line that goes up and down the map first (the numbers or letters along the bottom), then the line that goes from side to side (the numbers along the side). So Dimple is in square 2960.

## Look at the map

→ Look carefully at the map of Matlock, which is on the River Derwent, in Derbyshire. The River Derwent is the longest river in the Peak District. Answer these questions about the map.

→ What is the name of the station nearest to the river?

→ What runs alongside most of the river?

→ Where is the best place to drive across the river?

→ Where would a tourist be able to find information about the area?

→ Where is the biggest river meander? Give a grid reference to this square on the map.

→ Why do you think most of the settlement is on the north side of the river?

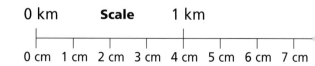

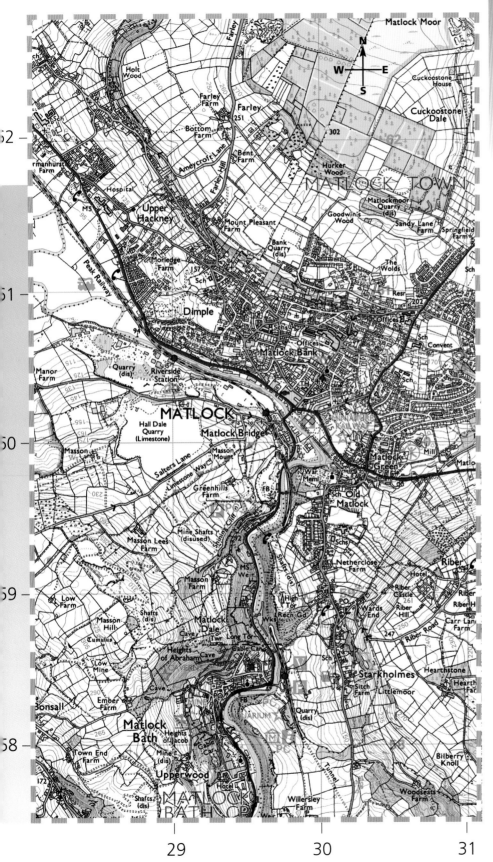

## Map Key

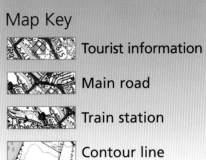

Tourist information

Main road

Train station

Contour line

## SYMBOLS

Map symbols bring a map to life. They are simple signs that show where things are on a map. A list called a key or a legend on the edge of the map explains what the symbols stand for.

## HEIGHT

The ups and downs of the land can be shown on a flat map by pictures of hills, shading, coloured areas or lines called hachures. The main way of showing height on a map is usually by contour lines. These are brown lines that join up places that are the same height above sea level. When the contours are close together, the land is steep. When the contours are far apart, the land is flatter. Rings of contours, one inside the other, show hills or mountains.

# Britain's rivers

This map shows some of the major rivers of Britain. It also shows all the rivers mentioned in this book.

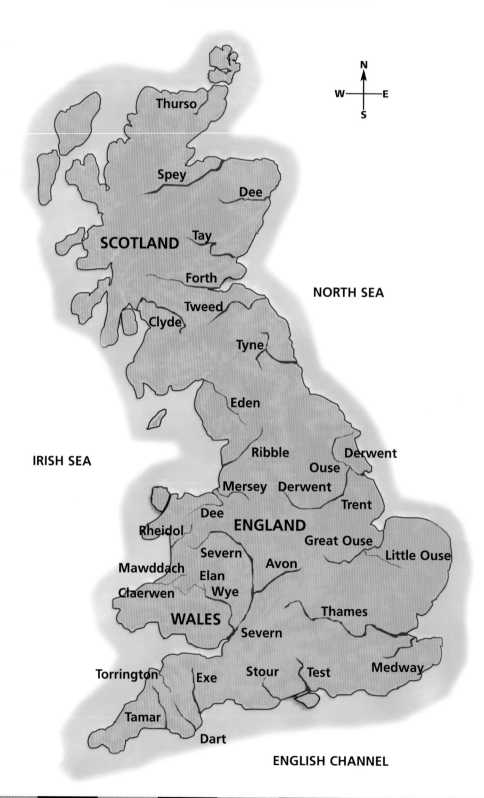

N
W — E
S

Thurso

Spey

Dee

SCOTLAND  Tay

Forth

NORTH SEA

Tweed

Clyde

Tyne

Eden

IRISH SEA

Ribble  Derwent

Ouse

Mersey  Derwent

Trent

Dee  ENGLAND

Rheidol

Great Ouse

Severn  Avon

Little Ouse

Mawddach  Elan

Claerwen  Wye

Thames

WALES

Severn

Torrington  Exe  Stour  Test  Medway

Tamar

Dart

ENGLISH CHANNEL

# Glossary

**Atlas** A book of maps.

**Aerial photograph** A photograph taken from the sky looking down on the land.

**Canal** A man-made waterway (often fairly straight) used for transport or watering crops.

**Condensation** The process by which a gas (such as water vapour) changes into a liquid (such as liquid water) when it cools down.

**Contour** A line on a map which joins places that are the same height above sea level.

**Dam** A large wall or bank built across a river to hold back the water.

**Drainage pattern** The arrangement of a river and its tributaries across the land, seen from above.

**Erosion** The loosening of rocks and soil and the carrying away of this material by the wind, water or ice.

**Estuary** The wide mouth of a river where freshwater in the river mixes with the salty water of the sea.

**Evaporation** The process by which a liquid changes into a gas (such as water vapour) when it is heated.

**Ferry** A place where people or goods are carried across water, such as a river, in a boat.

**Floodplain** The wide, flat valley floor of a lowland river, which is often flooded by the river water.

**Ford** A shallow area of water that may be crossed by wading, riding or driving through the water.

**Gill** A narrow mountain stream or a deep valley.

**Glacier** A large mass of ice on high ground, which flows slowly downhill.

**Great Britain** A country that includes England, Wales and Scotland.

**Grid lines** Lines forming a network of squares on a map, which help to locate points on the map easily and accurately.

**Hachure** A short, thick line used on maps to show the steepness and direction of slopes.

**Hydro-power** Electrical power generated by water making turbine wheels move. ("Hydro" means water.)

**Key** A list that explains what the symbols on a map stand for. A key is sometimes called a legend because it tells the story of the map.

**Lock** A narrow section of a river with gates at either end. Inside the lock, boats can be raised or lowered by changing the water level.

**Meander** A large bend or loop in the course of a river, named after the River Meander in Turkey.

**Megalitre** One million litres.

**Mouth** The end of a river, where it flows into the sea or a lake.

**Ordnance Survey** An organisation that makes accurate and detailed maps of the UK.

**Precipitation** All forms of water falling out of clouds to the Earth including rain, snow, hail and sleet.

**Reservoir** A lake made when people dam a river. A reservoir stores water for drinking, watering crops or making electricity.

**Scale** The number of units of measurement on the ground represented by a certain number of units on a map.

**Sediment** Small particles of rocks, soil or living things that are carried along and deposited (dropped) by the river.

**Settlement** A place where people build their homes and settle down to live their lives.

**Spot height** A point on a map where the exact height of the land is marked.

**Spring** A place where water comes up to the surface and pours out to form a stream.

**Tarn** A small lake.

**Tributary** A small stream or river that flows into a bigger stream or river.

**Waterfall** A point where a river suddenly drops over a "step" of rock and forms a curtain of falling water.

**Weir** A dam across a river to regulate the flow of water.

# Index

## FURTHER INFORMATION WEBSITES:

### Websites on maps
Ordnance Survey: www.ordnancesurvey.co.uk/mapzone
www.multimap.co.uk
Type in place names or postcodes to see aerial views and maps of places in Britain.

### Websites about the environment:
Sustainable cities: www.sustainable-cities.org.uk
Environment Agency: www.environment-agency.gov.uk
The National Trust: www.nationaltrust.org.uk

### Websites about rivers:
http://woodlands-junior.kent.sch.uk/riverthames/facts.htm
www.york.gov.uk/leisure/rivers/
www.marlowtown.co.uk/marlhist.html
www.timbosliverpool.co.uk/mersey/index.htm
www.theclydebankstory.com/story_TCSC03.php
www.bbc.co.uk/wales/mid/sites/history/pages/facts.shtml
www.vagavalley.co.uk/elan_valley.htm
www.bbc.co.uk/devon/discovering/rivers/torridge/shtml
www.tarka-country.co.uk/tarkatrust/tarkaott.html
www.derbyshireuk.net/river derwent.html
www.sln.org.uk/trentweb/newpage31.htm

These are the lists of contents for each title in
*Mapping Britain's Landscapes:*